Jacob and Esau

Story by Penny Frank
Illustrated by Tony Morris

CARMEL • NEW YORK 10512

The Bible tells us how God chose the Israelites to be his special people. He made them a promise that he would always love and care for them. But they must obey him.

The founder of God's special nation was a man called Abraham.

This story is about Abraham's son, Isaac, and his family. They had to learn to obey and trust God as Abraham did.

You can find the story in your own Bible, in Genesis, chapters 27 to 33.

Copyright © 1986 Lion Publishing

Published by
Lion Publishing plc
Icknield Way, Tring, Herts, England
ISBN 0 85648 731 7
Lion Publishing Corporation
1705 Hubbard Avenue, Batavia,
Illinois 60510, USA
ISBN 0 85648 731 7
Albatross Books Pty Ltd
PO Box 320, Sutherland, NSW 2232, Australia
ISBN 0 86760 515 4

First edition 1986
Reprinted 1986

Printed and bound in Hong Kong by Mandarin Offset International (HK) Ltd
This Guideposts edition is published by special arrangement with Lion Publishing

British Library Cataloguing in Publication Data

Frank, Penny
Jacob and Esau. – (The Lion Story Bible; 6)
1. Esau – Juvenile literature 2. Jacob –
Juvenile literature
3. Bible stories, English – O.T.
Genesis
I. Title   II. Morris, Tony
222'.11'0922   BS580.E65

ISBN 0-85648-731-7

Library of Congress Cataloging in Publication Data

Frank, Penny.
Jacob and Esau.
(The Lion Story Bible; 6)
1. Jacob (Biblical patriarch) –
Juvenile literature.
2. Esau (Biblical figure) – Juvenile
literature.
3. Bible. O.T. – Biography – Juvenile
literature.
[1. Jacob (Biblical patriarch). 2. Esau
(Biblical figure). 3. Bible stories – O.T.]
I. Morris, Tony, ill. II. Title. III. Series:
Frank, Penny. Lion Story Bible; 6.
BS580.J3F72 1986   222'.1109505
85-13129
ISBN 0-85648-731-7

Isaac lived in the land of Canaan.

He was old and blind. His wife
Rebecca looked after him.

Their sons were twins called Esau
and Jacob. They loved them both very
much.

When they were little boys, Esau and
Jacob enjoyed playing together.

There was always plenty to do around
the tent where they lived. There were
hills to climb and donkeys to ride.

But as they grew older they started to enjoy different things.

'Let's go out hunting for meat,' Esau would say.

But Jacob would answer, 'No thanks. I'd rather stay at home.'

Rebecca loved Jacob best. She was glad
that he stayed at home. They talked
together as they worked.

Jacob knew that even though they
were twins, Isaac would give Esau all
the special blessings of God kept for the
first son, because he was born first.

'It's just not fair,' Jacob would say to
his mother.

Isaac was glad that Esau loved hunting.
He enjoyed eating the meat Esau
caught, while he listened to his stories.
He loved to hear about the hills and the
fields and the world he could not see.

One day when Esau was out hunting,
Rebecca called to Jacob.

'Quickly, go and put on some of
Esau's clothes. We will make your father
give you the special blessing before Esau
comes back.'

Rebecca tied goatskins around Jacob's arms, to make them feel hairy, like Esau's. Then Jacob took some food to his father.

Isaac was blind, so he put out his hand to touch his son.

'Is that you, Esau?' he asked.

'Yes, father,' said Jacob, making his voice like Esau's.

So Isaac gave Jacob the special blessing of God, kept for the first son.

Jacob and Rebecca were glad. They knew now that Jacob would be a rich man. Isaac's blessing promised him a long life and success.

Then Esau came in from hunting. He
cooked the meat and took it in to his
father.

Esau asked his father for the special
blessing. Then Isaac knew he had been
tricked.

'You are too late, my dear son,' he told
Esau.

Esau was furious when he heard what had happened.

'My brother is a cheat. *I* should have God's special blessing. Please give it to me,' he begged.

'I can't,' said Isaac sadly. 'I gave it to Jacob and I cannot take it back.'

'I will kill him,' said Esau.

Rebecca heard what Esau said. So she sent Jacob away.

'Go and stay in the land where my brother lives,' she said. 'I will send you a message when it is safe for you to come home.'

So Jacob began his journey to Haran. It was a very long way.

When night-time came, he was tired. He found a dry place on the ground and used a big smooth stone as a pillow.

As he slept, he had a dream.

He dreamed of angels on a stairway going up to the sky.

He heard a voice say, 'I am the God of Abraham and Isaac. I will be with you on your journey, and bring you safely home.'

Jacob knew that God hated his cheating, and he was very afraid. But God had said he would keep the promise he had made to Abraham for his whole family.

In Haran Jacob found his uncle, Laban. He worked hard for him for many years, though Laban was a bigger cheat than Jacob!

Jacob became a rich man with sheep
and goats of his own. He wanted to
marry Laban's beautiful daughter,
Rachel. But Laban tricked him into
marrying her older sister.

Brother Esau stayed in Canaan. He felt
cheated and sad. Isaac and Rebecca
both died. But Esau worked hard.

He had a family and they lived in a big tent.

He often thought, 'I wish I knew where Jacob was. I would like to see him again.'

One day God told Jacob to travel back to Canaan, the land God had promised to Jacob's grandfather, Abraham.

Jacob took his family and animals with him.

Jacob was afraid of meeting Esau.

'I do not deserve the care and love you have shown me all these years,' he said to God. 'But please take care of me now, as I meet Esau.'

Jacob sent presents of sheep and goats
ahead of him, in case his brother was
still angry.

But Esau ran to meet Jacob. He threw
his arms around him and kissed him —
he was so glad Jacob had come back.

22

God had helped Esau to forgive Jacob. He had kept his promise to bring Jacob home, safe and sound. The two brothers were friends again.

The Story Bible Series from Guideposts is made up of 50 individual stories for young readers, building up an understanding of the Bible as one story—God's story—a story for all time and all people.

The Old Testament story books tell the story of a great nation—God's chosen people, the Israelites—and God's love and care for them through good times and bad. The stories are about people who knew and trusted God. From this nation came one special person, Jesus Christ, sent by God to save all people everywhere.

The New Testament story books cover the life and teaching of God's Son, Jesus. The stories are about the people he met, what he did and what he said. Almost all we know about the life of Jesus is recorded in the four Gospels—Matthew, Mark, Luke and John. The word gospel means 'good news.'

The last four stories in this section are about the first Christians, who started to tell others the 'good news,' as Jesus had commanded them—a story which continues today all over the world.

The story of *Jacob and Esau* comes from the first book of the Bible, Genesis, chapters 27–33. The two boys were twins, the grandsons of Abraham, whom God chose to be the founder of his special people. Isaac, their father, loved Esau best; Rebecca, their mother, loved Jacob best. And so she helped Jacob to cheat his brother of the rights which belonged to him as the elder son.

The Bible is not simply about good people. It is about people like Jacob, and like us, whom God still loves and whose lives he can change if only they will trust and obey him.